612.8   Parker, Steve.
PAR
         Touching a nerve.

$16.29   33197000018338

DATE			
T			

Touching a Nerve

How you touch, sense and feel

Steve Parker

FRANKLIN WATTS

New York • London • Toronto • Sydney

Franklin Watts, Inc.
95 Madison Avenue
New York, NY 10016

Printed in Great Britain

Library of Congress Cataloging-in-Publication Data
Parker, Steve.
    Touching a nerve / by Steve Parker.
      p.   cm. — (The body in action)
    Includes bibliographical references and index.
    Summary: Discusses the sense of touch and the process by which the
skin and the brain work together to register sensations.
    ISBN 0-531-14215-9
    1. Touch—Juvenile literature.   [1. Touch.   2. Senses and
sensation.]   I. Title.   II. Series.
QP451.P37   1992
612.8'8—dc20   91-39125
                                                                               CIP AC

Medical consultant: Dr. Puran Ganeri, MBBS, MRCP,
MRCGP, DCH

Series editors: Anita Ganeri and A. Patricia Sechi
Design: K and Co.
Illustrations: Rhoda and Robert Burns/Drawing Attention
Photography: Chris Fairclough
Typesetting: Lineage Ltd. Watford

The publisher would like to thank Andeep Patel for
appearing in the photographs of this book.

CONTENTS

Senses in action

You get information about your surroundings through your senses. Your eyes see and your ears hear. Your nose smells, and your tongue tastes. Your other main sense is touch. Your skin can feel all kinds of touches – pressure, texture, movement, and pain too!

△ When you get ready to go out, you use your sense of touch in many ways. Can you tie your shoelaces without looking at what you are doing? Your fingers feel the laces and move them into the right place.

▷ The parts of your body that sense your surroundings are called sense organs. Most of your sense organs are in your head. But the sense organ for touch is skin, which covers your whole body.

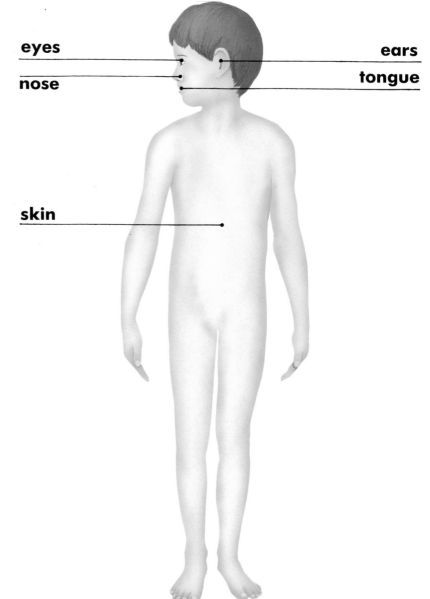

eyes

nose

ears

tongue

skin

4

TOUCH FACTS

- Think about all the things you can feel with your skin. Your sense of touch is much more complicated than it seems.
- You can feel different textures, from rough sandpaper to fine, smooth silk.
- With your skin you can feel different degrees of hardness or softness, from a hard pebble or stone to a soft sponge or piece of cotton fabric.
- An expert typist can touch the keys on a keyboard accurately without even looking at them. This is partly due to the body's inner sense of position, which is explained below.

A SENSE OF POSITION

Apart from your main senses, you can also sense the position of your body without having to look. Stretch detectors in your muscles and joints are constantly sending signals to your brain. They tell it whether your limbs and body are straight or bent. This is your proprioceptive, or kinesthetic, sense.

Try to sense the position of your fingers and arms. Close your eyes and hold your hands by your sides.

Point your forefingers toward each other. Can you touch fingertips? Try again if you don't succeed the first time. Do you get better with practice? How hard do you have to concentrate?

Inside your skin

Your sense of touch is really a "multisense." Your skin contains millions of nerves that are tiny sensors. Each kind sends its own signals to your brain. You feel a certain sensation from the sensor's position on your body, and the type of signals it sends. One sensation is light touch. Another is heavy pressure. Your skin can also detect heat and cold and much smaller changes in temperature, too. It also warns you of damage being done or about to be done to your body by making you feel pain.

△ You are ready to go out, but where is the baseball cap you had on earlier? Some places are difficult to get a good look inside, so you must feel around for the cap.

▷ This is what your skin looks like under a microscope. The outer layer is called the epidermis. It is made of hard, dead cells. Your touch sensors are in the living layer beneath it, called the dermis.

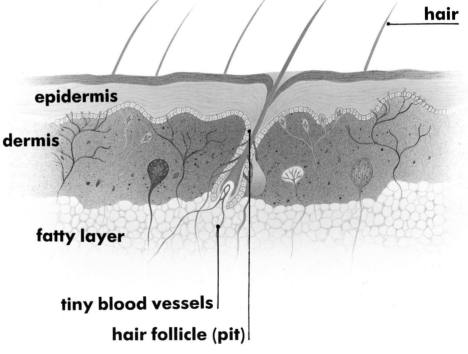

hair

epidermis

dermis

fatty layer

tiny blood vessels

hair follicle (pit)

6

HOW SENSITIVE IS YOUR SKIN?

Your skin is not equally sensitive all over. Touch sensors are packed closely together in some parts of your body, but are spread out in others.

You can test how sensitive various parts of the body are on a blindfolded friend. Tape a sharp pencil on to a ruler, as shown. Tape another pencil about ½ inch away. Touch your friend's skin with both points at the same time. Does she or he feel one point or two? If one, widen the gap between the pencils. If two, lessen it. Make a sensitivity map for various parts of the body, showing the smallest gap which can still be felt as two separate points. Tightly-packed touch sensors in your fingertips detect a gap of only 1 or 2 millimeters. In the middle of your back, though, the gap may be several inches wide.

SKIN FACTS

• The skin is one of the body's largest organs. The skin of an average adult covers an area of about 2½ square yards. It can weigh about 6½-9 pounds.
• Skin keeps out wind, water and germs, but keeps body fluids in.
• Skin is durable and is continually renewing itself.

• Skin cells at the base of the epidermis multiply, moving upward slowly and become hardened and tough. They replace older cells that are rubbed off. This journey takes about a month.
• Some animals have much thicker skin than us. A rhino's skin is over 2½ inches thick. It gives protection, but is not very flexible.

Delicate touch

△ Your fingers gently touch something that feels soft like the cap, and you pull it out to have a look. But it's only a long-lost tennis ball!

One type of skin sensor responds mainly to light touch. It is called Meissner's corpuscle. It is a tiny, oval-shaped object made of cells and fibers. Each of these sensors has fibers that carry nerve signals to your brain. If a sensor is squeezed or stretched slightly, it changes the pattern of signals it sends. You have millions of these sensors in your skin. They are most common in hairless skin, such as that on your palms and on your fingertips.

▷ Meissner's corpuscles are found in the upper part of the dermis, just below the epidermis. They are able to detect the slightest touch or movement on the surface just above them.

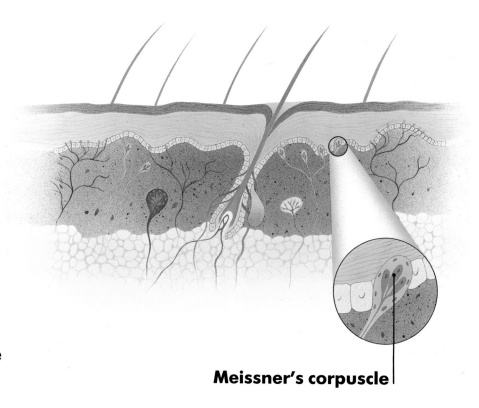

Meissner's corpuscle

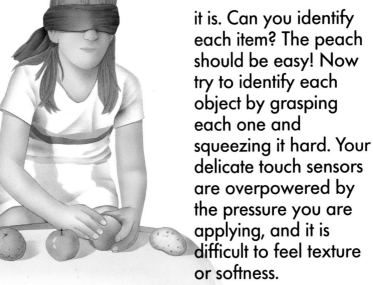

Test your sense of delicate touch with some things like an orange, a peach, an apple and a potato. Arrange these on a tray. With a friend to help, blindfold yourself and gently feel each of the things in turn. Stroke the object to detect its texture, and squeeze it carefully to feel how soft or spongy it is. Can you identify each item? The peach should be easy! Now try to identify each object by grasping each one and squeezing it hard. Your delicate touch sensors are overpowered by the pressure you are applying, and it is difficult to feel texture or softness.

THE SENSITIVE PERSON

This is what you would look like if each part of your body was drawn in proportion to how sensitive it is to touch! Parts with lots of sensors packed into a small area, such as your lips and fingertips, are very sensitive to touch. These are drawn big. Parts with fewer sensors in a larger area are drawn small, like your back and legs. Does this agree with your map from page 7?

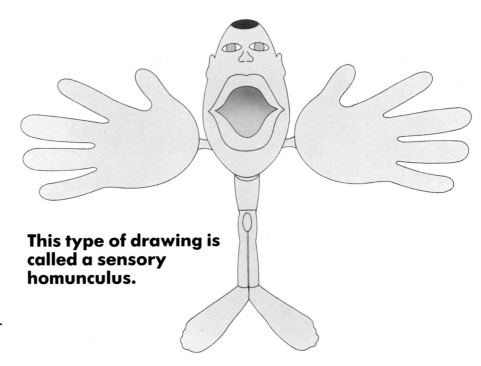

This type of drawing is called a sensory homunculus.

Under pressure

A second type of skin sensor responds mainly to heavy touch, or pressure. This is known as a Pacinian corpuscle. Like the Meissner's corpuscle, its nerve signals change when it is pressed or stretched. Pacinian corpuscles are bigger than Meissner's corpuscles, the largest being 2 millimeters long and half a millimeter wide. They are most common in such places as your hands, feet, arms, neck and chest.

△ Where is that cap? You're sure you put it somewhere sensible. You feel in the back of the drawer to find it, using the sense of heavy pressure in your fingers and hand.

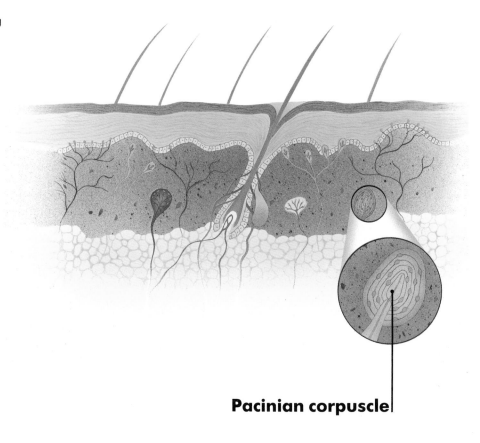

Pacinian corpuscle

▷ Pacinian corpuscles are found in the lower part of the dermis or the fatty layer just beneath. Being more deeply buried, they are not as sensitive as Meissner's corpuscles.

RESPONDING TO PRESSURE

The skin on the undersides of your feet is thicker than skin elsewhere. The epidermis (the hardened, mostly dead, outer layer) is especially thick, four millimeters or more. This gives protection from the great pressure of your whole body weight, as you walk, run and jump. Have you spent much time not wearing shoes, perhaps on vacation

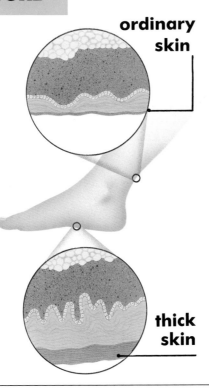

ordinary skin

thick skin

on the beach? Your bare feet may be sore at first; but after a few days, the skin on the undersides of your feet grows thicker, to protect itself against the greater rubbing and wear. The skin on your hands can also grow thicker for protection. Specially thickened patches of skin are called calluses. They may also form if your shoe constantly rubs on part of your foot.

LOOKING AT TOUGH SPOTS

If you regularly press or grip hard with your hands and fingers, you may have specially thickened skin at the pressure points. People who play the guitar develop hard skin on the ends of their fingertips, where they press the strings. People who play a lot of tennis or squash may have tough skin on their fingers and palms

where they grip the racket. Look at the palms and fingers of someone who uses her or his hands a lot, like a builder, mechanic or gardener. Do they have calluses where the wear and pressure on the skin is greatest? What about people who use their hands in a less physical way, such as computer operators or teachers?

11

Ouch! That hurt!

△ You close the drawer, taking care not to trap your fingers in it. Last time, you shut your finger in it and had to have a bandage put on the painful cut.

Another type of sensor in your skin makes you feel pain. It is called a free nerve ending and is made of the bare ends of a nerve fiber. They branch out into the upper part of the dermis. These sensors are dotted all over your skin. They are also in many of your internal parts, such as your muscles and joints. They change the pattern of signals they send to your brain, when your body is about to be injured or damaged, or has been hurt already.

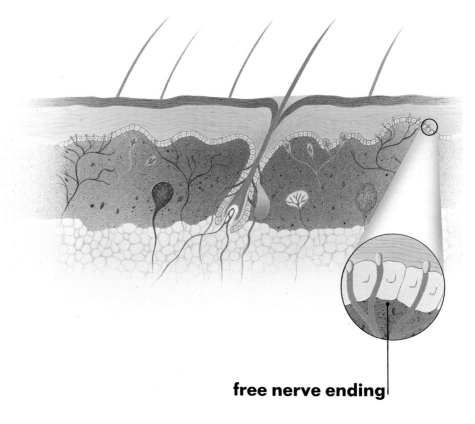

▷ The free nerve endings are mostly in the upper part of your dermis, branching out toward the epidermis. They send pain signals to warn you of injury or damage.

free nerve ending

PAIN FACTS

- The pain sensors on your fingers are only 2 or 3 millimeters apart. On your thigh, however, they may be over 2 inches apart.
- People describe different kinds of pain. It may be sharp, dull or aching, throbbing or stabbing.
- A patient who can describe pain accurately can help their doctor a great deal. From a good description of the pain,

and where it is in the body, the doctor can figure out what is wrong. They can then prescribe medicines to ease the pain.
- Moods and emotions may affect how much pain you feel. When you are feeling nervous or anxious about something, you may feel pain more severely than if you were relaxed.

CONTROLLING PAIN

Some people can control or block out pain, using the power of mind over matter. They can put themselves into a kind of trance, and can then walk on hot coals or lie on a bed of nails without getting hurt. Don't try this for yourself! It takes years of practice. Natural body chemicals, called endorphins, seem to be able to lessen pain. In medicine, a local anesthetic is used to "deaden" part of the body, so you feel no sensations (including pain) there. A general anesthetic puts you to sleep, so you feel no sensations at all.

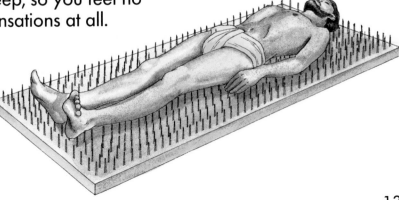

Keeping out germs

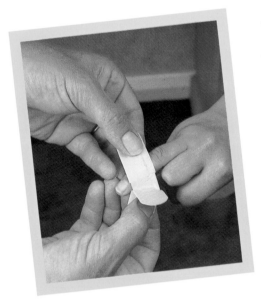

Yet another of your skin's many uses is to keep out germs that could make you ill. The outer surface of the epidermis is made of layers of tiny, dead, flattened cells. They overlap like roof tiles to form a continuous covering, which can keep out even the smallest germs. Your skin's natural oils and waxes also help to keep out or kill germs.

△ A clean bandage helps to keep germs out of a cut, until the skin heals over it.

▷ From the moment it is cut (1), your skin works to close the wound and repair itself. First, the blood clots to make a temporary seal (2). Then fibers form and knit the sides of the gash together (3). Gradually, new skin cells grow from the bottom to the top of the gap, and complete the repair (4).

1 | **fresh cut**

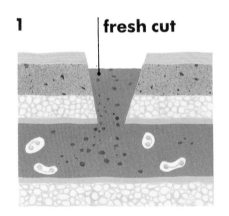

2 | **blood clot**

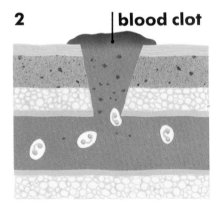

3 | **fibers**

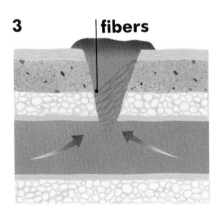

4 | **new skin**

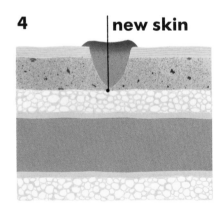

WHAT ARE BRUISES?

A bruise is caused by bleeding under the skin. A hard knock or blow breaks the blood vessels and blood leaks into the surrounding area. The blood is dark red at first because of the pigment (coloring), hemoglobin. This normally carries oxygen around your body. But it turns blue

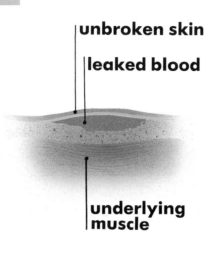

unbroken skin

leaked blood

underlying muscle

as it loses its oxygen and goes "stale." Gradually, the broken blood vessels repair themselves. The stale hemoglobin is broken down into yellow or green pigments and the bruise changes color. The leaked blood causes painful pressure at first, but this fades as it is cleaned away.

HOW TO CLEAN A WOUND

Always clean cuts or grazes with soap and water to remove dirt and germs. Dab a cotton ball with an antiseptic. Wipe it gently on the cut, cleaning away from the cut (1). Dry the area with more cotton (2). Cover the cut with a butterfly bandage or small bandage (3). Change the bandage regularly so that it does not get dirty.

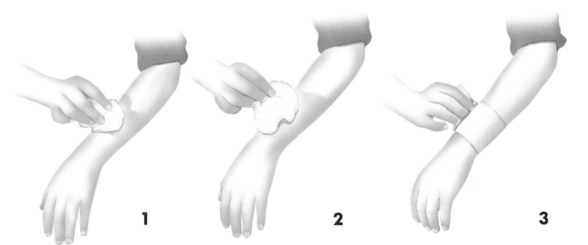

1　　　**2**　　　**3**

KEEPING SKIN CLEAN

Even normal, healthy skin has hundreds of tiny germs and other living things on it. Keeping your skin clean means it is less likely to become infected by the germs or develop blackheads and pimples. It is especially important to keep your hands clean. They touch many parts of your body, your food, clothes and other items. Dirty hands can spread germs. Wash your hands with soap and warm water. Rinse them, then dry them on a clean towel. Do this after using the bathroom, before meals and before handling food.

BLEMISH FACTS

• A birthmark is a patch of skin that has more (or less) colored pigment in it, compared to the skin around it. Or it may have different types of blood vessels, which make it look different. These marks are present from birth.

• A mole is an area of dark skin, containing more of the natural skin coloring, melanin.

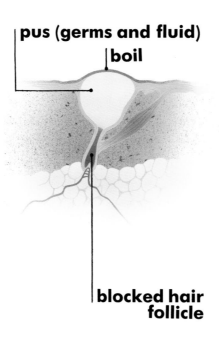

pus (germs and fluid)

boil

blocked hair follicle

• A blackhead is a plug of dark material (sometimes dirt) and natural skin oils, blocking a tiny pore (natural hole) in the skin.

• A boil is a red inflammation caused by the infection of a hair follicle by germs. Boils can be very painful.

• A wart is a small lump caused by infection by viruses, which are types of germs.

Your nails

△ The drawer is stuck, but you can feel how hard you are gripping it by the pressure on your fingertips and fingernails. Where *can* that cap be?

Each fingernail and toenail grows from a specialized part of the skin called, the nail root. The thin skin around the nail edge is called the cuticle. The nail grows slowly and continuously toward the tip of the finger or toe. It is joined to the skin beneath, known as the nail bed. A nail is almost transparent, but it looks pink due to the tiny blood vessels and skin under it. Nails may help your sense of touch by forming hard, rigid pads behind the sensitive fingertips. This gives each fingertip something to support it, as you press and prod things to find their hardness.

▷ At the root of your nail, a patch of skin folds back on itself. It wraps around the part from where the nail grows. The pale part beyond the cuticle is called the lunula.

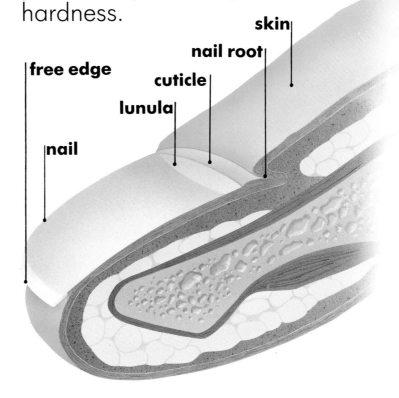

skin

nail root

cuticle

free edge

lunula

nail

NAIL FACTS

- A nail grows about 1 millimeter a week. Fingernails grow a bit faster than toenails.
- If you are right-handed, the nails on your right hand may grow slightly faster than those on your left.
- Most people's nails grow faster in summer than in winter.
- One man in India grew fingernails over 27½ inches long!

- The substance that gives nails their hardness is a protein called keratin.
- Keratin also gives skin its toughness, and forms the outer layer of your hair.
- Keratin also forms claws, hooves and horns. The sloth has long curved claws of keratin, which it uses to hang upside down from a branch all day.

PUTTING THE PRESSURE ON

Your fingertips and fingernails may help you to feel and apply just the right amount of pressure. Balance a ruler on a pencil eraser with a small weight at one end. Press down gently with your fingertip on the other end of the ruler, so that the weight slides along smoothly. You will be able to feel the weight resisting and starting to slide, through your finger. Now press the ruler with the back of your finger or your palm. Without the delicate "pressure gauge" of your fingertips pushing against your fingernails, it is difficult to move the weight along the ruler so smoothly.

18

NAIL CARE

Long nails can look good, but they must be cared for properly. Long nails can easily get dirty or split.

- Trim your nails every 2-3 weeks, with sharp, nail scissors, or special nail clippers.
- Use an emery (sandpaper) board or nail file to get rid of nicks or snags in the nail edge.
- Don't cut too far into the corners of toenails,

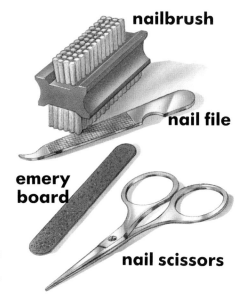

nailbrush

nail file

emery board

nail scissors

since this may damage the skin and cause ingrown toenails.

- Clean your nails with a nailbrush and soapy water, especially after handling dirty things.
- If your nails are painful, or the skin around them is red or swollen, tell your doctor. You may have an infection.
- Try not to bite your nails.

HOW SENSITIVE ARE YOUR NAILS?

Your nails cannot feel anything on their own. They are made of dead keratin, as is your hair and your skin's epidermis. But the dermis of the skin around and under your nails is very sensitive.

Balance one end of a bathroom scale on the table. Then grip the other end in your hand. Look at the dial to see how hard you can squeeze. Try your hands and fingers in various positions. When

you grip so that you press with your fingernails, this may hurt. You probably cannot squeeze very hard like this. You can put on more pressure with the fronts or sides of your fingers.

pressing with nail area

pressing with flats of fingers

pressing with whole hand

Touch on the brain

Every second, each inch of your skin sends thousands of nerve signals to your brain. They carry information about the "multisense" of touch. The signals arrive at a strap-shaped area of the brain, called the sensory cortex. It wraps over the top of the main part of your brain, called the cortex. Each patch of your sensory cortex gets signals from one part of your body. It analyzes and interprets them, and you "feel" them.

△ You *still* haven't found the cap. It must be nearby! To save moving all the clothes on the chair, you feel under it for the cap's shape and its texture.

▷ The sensory cortex is a narrow strip in the top part of the brain. Each part of it deals with signals coming from skin on a certain part of the body. Areas of skin that have many sensors, such as the fingers, have larger patches of cortex to deal with them.

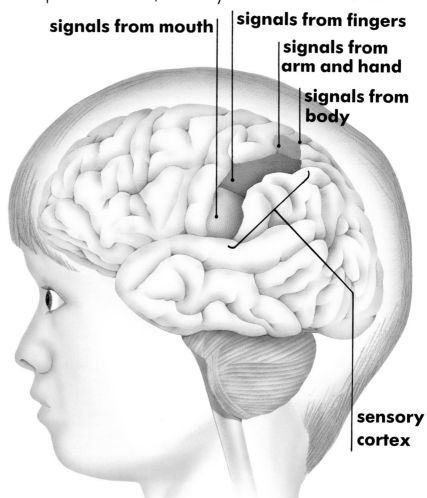

signals from mouth **signals from fingers**

signals from arm and hand

signals from body

sensory cortex

20

Optical illusions fool your eyes, but your sense of touch can also be tricked. Cross your first and second fingers, and grip a dried pea or small stone between them (as shown on the right). Look away. Does it feel more like two peas than one? When these two sides of your fingers feel something, there are usually two objects there (see far right).

TOUCH AND BRAIN FACTS

• Parts of your body that are very sensitive to touch, like your fingertips, send huge numbers of signals to your brain. They need a large area of sensory cortex to deal with them all.

• Nerve signals from the different types of sensors in your skin travel along their nerves to your brain at different speeds.

• Signals about a light touch speed along at about 150 miles an hour.

• Signals about a pinprick travel much more slowly — at about 25 miles an hour.

• Signals warning of pain travel at less than 2½ miles an hour.

• This is why, when you stub your toe, you feel the touch first. These signals travel fastest and reach your brain first. A split second later the pain signals arrive — ouch!

touch signal

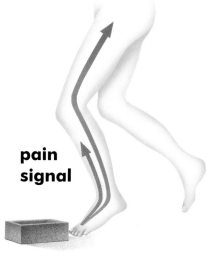
pain signal

Hot or cold?

If you go outside on a winter's day, you will feel cold air on your face. If you dip your toe into a warm bath, you will feel hot water on your foot. Part of your skin's "multisense" is being able to detect temperatures. One type of temperature sensor is called Krause's bulb. This may help to detect cold. The other type of sensor is called Ruffini's organ. It helps to detect heat, and perhaps heavy touch.

△ Ow! In your search for the cap, you forgot about the warm radiator hidden behind the chair! The hot feeling on your skin makes you pull your hands away at once.

▷ As with the other types of skin sensors, there are millions of temperature sensors dotted about in your skin. They are set deep in the dermis. Nerves connect them to your brain.

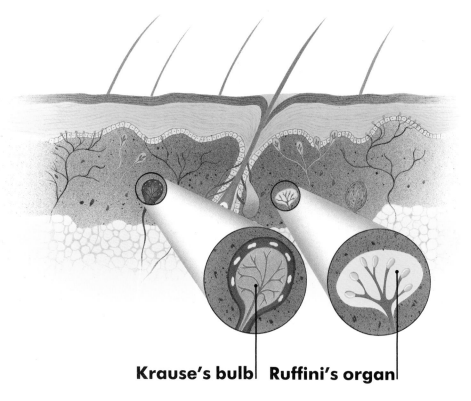

Krause's bulb **Ruffini's organ**

REFLEX FACTS

- A reflex is a fast automatic reaction of your body. Some reflexes are linked to feelings in the skin.
- If you detect a hot sensation in your skin, you jerk that part of your body away at once — even if you are concentrating on something else. This automatic reaction reduces your chances of being burned.

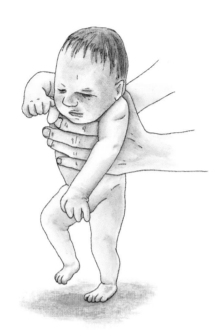

- If something touches your eye or the skin around it, you automatically close your eyelid and move your face back, out of harm's way.
- A newborn baby held over a firm surface makes stepping movements when its feet touch the surface. This "walking reflex" soon fades and the baby has to learn to walk.

TESTING TEMPERATURE

Sensitivity to heat or cold varies over your body. Use different areas of your skin to test the temperature of a bowl of warm water. Try with your elbow, your toes or your fingertip. With which does the water feel warmest? Check the water's real temperature with a thermometer.

Hairy skin

△ You are beginning to wonder if you will ever see your cap again. Deep in thought, you try to scratch the hair on your head — and your fingers feel a surprise!

You have up to 5 million hairs on your body. They grow all over, except on your palms, the fronts of your fingers, the soles of your feet and the bases of your toes. Each hair grows from a deep pit in your skin, called a follicle. Tiny cells at the base of the hair multiply, pushing the hair up through the follicle. The main part of the hair, called the shaft, is made of dead cells filled with the tough protein, keratin.

▷ In a hair follicle, the epidermis folds down into the dermis. At the side of the follicle is a sebaceous gland. This gland makes natural oily and waxy substances, to keep your skin and hair supple and waterproof.

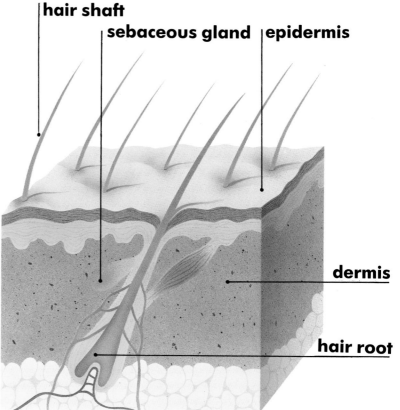

hair shaft

sebaceous gland **epidermis**

dermis

hair root

HOW STRONG IS YOUR HAIR?

For their thickness, hairs are very tough and strong. A single hair could hold up to 6 ounces. Try this test to see how strong a single hair is. Use a long hair, and tie one end to an S-shape hook and the other to a stick or bar. Hang a string or net bag on the other end of the hook. Gradually fill the bag one by one with marbles or similar small weights of about ½ ounce each.

How much weight can the hair hold before it snaps? This point is called its breaking point. Remember to weigh the empty bag and hook first. Test the suggestion that straight hair is stronger than curly, wavy or frizzy hair. See if the color of the hair affect its strength. Is hair stronger than very thin cotton thread, or thin fishing line, for example?

HAIRY FACTS

• You may not seem hairy, compared to animals such as orangutans. But you have about as many hairs as they do. The difference is that many of your hairs are smaller.
• A human hair grows about ½ inch each month.
• Yaks have very thick hair, over 3 feet long, to keep them warm.

• An average person has about 100,000 hairs on his or her head.

Ignoring your senses

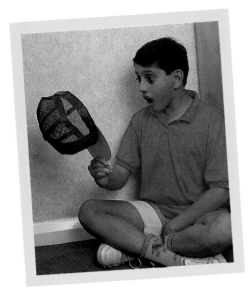

△ At last, you find your cap! You had forgotten that you put it on your head some time ago, and had become used to the feeling of it being there.

Your brain receives millions of nerve signals from your sense organs. It cannot analyze all of this information so it automatically filters most of it out. For example, the skin on your feet feels your socks when you first put them on. But after a while, you no longer notice them. The same happens with a watchband on your wrist, or a hat on your head. This process is called habituation. You get so used to a feeling that you no longer notice it.

skin with nothing on it

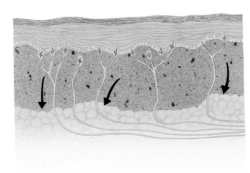

few nerve signals

▷ Every day, you put on clothes and other items. At first they send strong signals to your brain. Soon the signals fade as you get used to having the clothes on.

skin with sock just put on it

lots of nerve signals

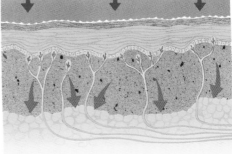

DOES IT ITCH?

Sometimes your skin may itch, even when there seems to be nothing there. A tiny speck of dust may be wedged in a hair follicle, or the hair could be bent over. Hairs have sensitive nerves wrapped around their roots and lower shafts. These detect even the slightest movement or pressure on the hair.

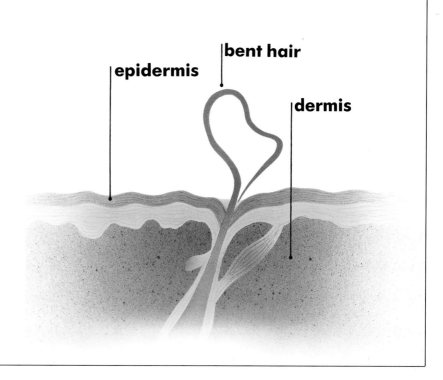

epidermis   **bent hair**   **dermis**

CHANGING TEMPERATURES

When you first get into a bath, it may feel very hot. But it soon feels cooler, even though the water temperature has hardly changed. This is because your skin's temperature sensors have become used to the water, and they send fewer signals to your brain. They send more signals again when the temperature changes. Try dipping a finger in lukewarm water for a minute and leave. Then put it in warmer water, which should feel slightly hotter.

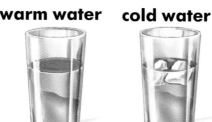

warm water   **cold water**

lukewarm water

Things to do

THE FEELY BOX

Can you identify objects just by feeling their shape and texture? Make a "feely box" from a cardboard box, with a hole cut in one end. Put a selection of objects inside and ask friends to feel and identify them.

FINGERPRINTS

The skin on your palms and the tips of your fingers has tiny ridges, that form patterns of waves and whorls. The ridges help you to grip and to feel textures and vibrations. The patterns are called fingerprints. Each person has different fingerprints. Look at yours by dabbing your fingers on an ink pad, then pressing them gently

on a piece of paper. Compare your prints to those of your friends. Jumble up prints of individual fingers, and try to group them back into hands by their pattern types.

28

HAIR SURVEY

Do a hair survey in your class. Copy this chart with colored crayons, ranging from blond hair through light brown and red, to dark brown and black. Hold it near each person's hair, to match the color. How many people have brown hair, for instance? Which is the most common hair color?

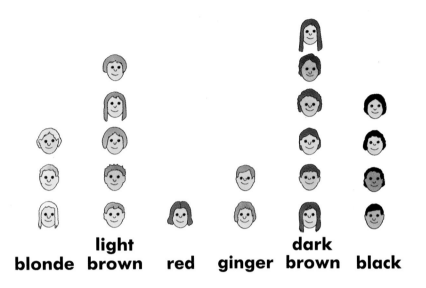

blonde **light brown** **red** **ginger** **dark brown** **black**

HAIR COUNT

It is said that an average of 70-100 hairs fall out of a person's head each day. Don't worry, new ones usually grow in their place! A typical hair lasts for 3 years before falling out and being replaced. Count your own hair loss by brushing your hair with a clean hairbrush in the morning and at night. Use a brush with well-spaced bristles, so that you can easily pull out and separate the hairs. Count how many hairs you lose over a week. Are you about average? You also lose hairs washing and on clothes and your pillow.

SKIN FACT

The amount of fat in the lower layers of skin varies from one person to another. In overweight people, it is usually greater. With your thumb and forefinger, gather and hold a fold of skin from your abdomen. How thick is it? About 3/4-1 inch is average. If fat has built up in the skin, the fold may well be thicker.

Glossary

Blood A red liquid that flows around the body inside tubes, called blood vessels. It carries nutrients and energy-containing substances from digested foods.

Brain A large, tangled mass of interconnected nerves inside the head. It is the control center of the body. Other nerves link it to the various parts of the body.

Dermis The lower layer of skin, below the epidermis. It contains skin sensors, blood vessels, nerves and elastic fibers.

Epidermis The outer surface layer of skin, above the dermis. It is mostly tough and dead, and resistant to wear and rubbing.

Follicle A deep "pit" in the skin, from which a hair grows.

Free nerve ending The bare, branched ends of a nerve in the skin. Free nerve endings mainly detect pain as well as heat.

Habituation When the sense organs and brain get used to something, so that you are no longer aware of it; for example, the feeling of a ring on the finger.

Kinesthetic sense See proprioceptive sense.

Meissner's corpuscle A microscopic rounded sensor in the skin. It mainly detects light touch.

Muscle A body part specialized for becoming shorter (contracting). As it does so, it pulls on the bone, muscle, or other body parts to which it is attached.

Nerve A long, thin bundle of neurons (nerve cells) that carries nerve signals from one part of the body to another.

Nerve signal A tiny electrical message that travels along a nerve. Nerve signals from the sense organs are carried along nerves to the brain, where they are analyzed and sorted out.

Pacinian corpuscle A microscopic rounded sensor in the skin. It mainly detects heavy pressure.

Pain A strong feeling of discomfort, hurt or distress. It usually warns that something is wrong or about to go wrong with the body.

Proprioceptive sense The inner sense of position, which causes you to "feel" the positions of your body and limbs, without having to look at them.

Sense organ A part of the body that detects some aspect of its surroundings, turns it into electrical nerve signals, and sends these along nerves to the brain for analysis.

Resources

BOOKS

The Neurological System **by Dale C. Garell and Solomon H. Snyder**
(New York: Chelsea House, 1989)

Messengers to the Brain: Your Fantastic Five Senses **by Paul D. Martin**
(Washington, D.C.: National Geographic Society, 1984)

Touch, Taste and Smell, rev. ed. **by Steve Parker**
(New York: Franklin Watts, 1989)

The Nerve Cell **by Diane D. Ralston and Henry J. Ralston III**
(North Carolina: Carolina Biological, 1988)

Understanding the Senses **by Graham Storrs**
(Needham Heights, Massachusetts: Silver Burdett & Ginn, 1985)

Index